NATIONAL GEOGRAPHIC

D0100644

What Makes a Tiger Hard to See?

Louis Capra

Some animals have coverings that make them hard to see. Their coverings blend in with their surroundings.

This tiger lives in the grasslands.

What makes the tiger hard to see?

The stripes on a tiger's fur help it blend in.
It is hard to see a tiger in the long grass.

This frog lives in a pond.

What makes the frog hard to see?

The frog's green skin helps it blend in.
It is hard to see a frog on a lily pad.

This snowshoe hare lives on a snowy mountain.

What makes the snowshoe hare hard to see?

The snowshoe hare's white fur helps it blend in.
It is hard to see a snowshoe hare in the snow.

This leopard lives in a forest.

What makes the leopard hard to see?

The spots on the leopard's fur help it blend in.
It is hard to see a leopard in the trees.

This sea dragon lives in the ocean.

What makes the sea dragon hard to see?

The shape of a sea dragon's body helps it blend in.
It is hard to see a sea dragon in the seaweed.

This gecko lives in the desert.

What makes the gecko hard to see?

The gecko's sandy-colored skin helps it blend in.
It is hard to see a gecko in the desert sand.

This owl lives in a tree.

What makes the owl hard to see?

The owl's speckled feathers help it blend in.
It is hard to see an owl in a tree.